HEALTH WATCH

Cerebral Palsy

JOHN COOPERSMITH GOLD

Expert Review by Stephen D. Rioux, M.D.

Enslow Publishers, Inc.

40 Industrial Road	PO Box 38
Box 398	Aldershot
Berkeley Heights, NJ 07922	Hants GU12 6BP
USA	UK

http://www.enslow.com

This book is dedicated to all who face special challenges in order to enjoy the most life has to offer. You have my admiration.

Acknowledgments
With thanks to: Stephen D. Rioux, M.D., director of Muscular Dystrophy Clinics in Maine and pediatric neurologist, for his advice and review of this book.
To Jennifer Decker and her family and to Shana Nelon and Austin Robertson for sharing their stories.

Printed in the United States of America.

Library of Congress Cataloging-in-Publication Data
Gold, John Coopersmith.
    Cerebral palsy / John Coopersmith Gold.
        p. cm.—(Health watch)
    Includes bibliographical references and index.
    ISBN 0-7660-1663-3 (hardcover)
    1. Cerebral palsy—Juvenile literature. [1. Cerebral palsy. 2. Diseases.]
[DNLM: 1. Cerebral Palsy—Popular Works. WS 342 G618c 2001] I. Title.
II. Health watch (Berkeley Heights, N.J.)
    RC388 .G645 2001
    616.8'36—dc21

$\mathcal{I}$

616.836

00-012882

10 9 8 7 6 5 4 3 2 1

GoL

$C. 1$

To Our Readers:
All Internet Addresses in this book were active and appropriate when we went to press. Any comments or suggestions can be sent by e-mail to Comments@enslow.com or to the address on the back cover.

Illustration and Photo Credits
Courtesy, Shana Nelon: pp. 1, 4, 7; © 1995-1997 Nova Development Corp.; pp. 6, 10; © Jill Gregory: p. 11; courtesy, the Decker-Carroll family, p. 12, 34, 37; © PhotoDisc: pp. 17, 19, 27; courtesy, National Cancer Institute: p. 20; © Candace Pratt Photography: p. 31.

Cover Illustrations
Large photo, courtesy, the Decker-Carroll family; top inset, © 1995-1997 Nova Development Corp.; bottom inset, courtesy, Shana Nelon.

Contents

CHAPTER 1

Austin's Story   5

CHAPTER 2

What Is Cerebral Palsy?   9

CHAPTER 3

Causes and Diagnosis   16

CHAPTER 4

Treatment   24

CHAPTER 5

Living With Cerebral Palsy   29

Further Reading   39
For More Information (with Internet Addresses)   41
Glossary   44
Index   47

Austin Robertson, four, enjoys a ride during the summer of 2000.

Austin's Story

At the age of two and one-half, Austin Robertson could draw a crowd around him. His bright blue eyes, blond hair, and engaging smile brought women from across a room to coo and admire. His mother, Shana Nelon, acknowledged that Austin liked to flirt.

"He is adorable. He's a cute kid," she said.

Austin, now four, is in many ways much like other children his age. But he has had to struggle to do things that other children do easily, like talk, walk, or feed himself. When his friends began speaking in sentences, Austin could use only single words. Sometimes he could only grunt and point to what he wanted. As Austin grew older, his speech improved. "There is no limit to the words that are coming out of his mouth," his mother said.

But Austin still cannot walk or sit by himself. He cannot stand on his own without leaning on something for support. His physical abilities are about the same as a child who is five months old.

Austin has **cerebral palsy**. Cerebral palsy is an incurable disorder caused by brain damage to unborn or newly born children. The damage affects the part of the brain that controls the body's **muscles**.

Children with cerebral palsy grow more slowly than other children. They may have trouble walking. When cerebral palsy is severe enough to interfere with people's ability to walk, they may have to spend the rest of their life in a wheelchair. They may not be able to eat by themselves or talk

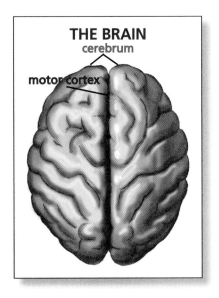

THE BRAIN
cerebrum
motor cortex

The motor cortex, a thin strip running from one end of the cerebrum to the other, controls the muscles. The left motor cortex controls the muscles in the right side of the body, while the right motor cortex controls the muscles in the body's left side.

and may be unable to care for themselves. Cerebral palsy does not go away as the child gets older.

In the United States, there are about five hundred thousand people with cerebral palsy. About two children in one thousand are born with the disorder.

Austin was born ten weeks earlier than expected. When he was born, he weighed only three pounds, about one-half the normal weight of most newborn children in the United States.

As Austin grew older, his mother noticed he wasn't

doing some of the activities other children his age could do. He didn't try to lift his head, sit up, or roll around. His mother realized that something might be wrong. During the next few months, she took him to several doctors. Finally, when Austin was nine months old, a doctor told his mother that Austin had cerebral palsy.

Austin's cerebral palsy affects his arms, his legs, and the muscles in his mouth. The disorder made it difficult for Austin to talk, chew, and swallow.

Austin Robertson, four, builds a snowman at his daycare program.

"It took so much effort for him to control his mouth that it was hard for him to talk," his mother said of Austin after his **diagnosis**.

Austin's diagnosis ended months of waiting and began what will be a lifetime of coping for him and his family. Twice a week Austin goes to a **physical therapist**, who stretches Austin's leg and arm muscles. Physical therapists use special exercises and equipment to help patients who have problems with movement. The physical therapist also teaches Austin's mother how to do stretching exercises with Austin at home.

Austin visited a **speech therapist**. This expert taught

him how to speak more clearly. The therapist also helped Austin and his mother find new ways to communicate with each other.

Austin attends a development group with other children who have cerebral palsy. In the group, therapists teach the children how to deal with their disabilities. The therapists showed Austin exercises to help him gain control over his right hand.

Although Austin has physical problems, he is "as normal and as smart as any toddler," his mother said. He loves to play with other children, although he is sometimes left behind when the children move around too quickly.

Austin has a board with pictures of everyday objects on it that he used to communicate with his mother when he was younger. It was also useful for the teachers and therapists who worked with Austin and for friends who wanted to communicate with him. When Austin wanted something, he pointed to a picture of the object.

Austin's mother says she is learning how to communicate better with her son. "Ninety-eight percent of the time I know what he is looking for," she says. "Because I'm his mom, I usually get it right."

Chapter 2

What Is Cerebral Palsy?

C erebral palsy was first described in the 1860s by an English surgeon named William Little. Little wrote about a disorder that caused stiff muscles in children and prevented them from walking, crawling, and grasping objects. The name cerebral palsy spells out the core features of the disorder. Cerebral refers to the brain. Palsy refers to a disorder that affects movement or posture.

Muscles are essential to living a normal life. Muscles allow people to move in all kinds of ways. We need muscles to talk because the muscles move the mouth and tongue. Muscles allow people to see by moving the eyes. When a person wiggles his or her finger, the muscles are at work. Muscles also help shape a person's body. They hold the bones of the skeleton in the right alignment, so that the feet point forward and the back stays straight.

A muscle is a piece of tissue in the body that connects bones and other tissues. The muscle is made up of many fibers that lie next to each other and can slide back and forth. The muscle works by contracting (becoming shorter) and expanding (becoming longer). When the muscle contracts, the bones or tissues that the muscle connects are pulled closer to each other. When the muscle expands or relaxes, the bones and tissue return to their original position.

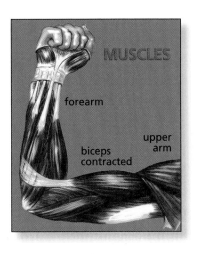

The biceps muscle contracts into a lump as it moves the forearm and the upper arm closer together.

A person can feel this happening when he or she "makes a muscle" by bending the arm at the elbow. When the person tightens the muscle, he or she can feel a lump grow on the upper arm. This lump is the biceps muscle making itself shorter as it brings the forearm bone and upper arm bone together. The lump forms when the muscle changes shape as it contracts.

When a person straightens the arm, the biceps muscle relaxes and the lump disappears. Another muscle underneath the arm contracts to straighten the arm.

The muscles are controlled by the brain, which is connected to the muscles by nerves. Nerves are the body's communications network, carrying signals from the brain to the rest of the body. When a person wants to move his or her arm, the brain sends a signal through the nerves to the biceps muscle. This causes the muscle to contract. At the same time, the brain also sends another signal, this one to the muscle underneath the arm, telling it to relax.

It often takes many different muscles to do things as simple as chewing or reaching out to push a button. All these muscles have to contract or relax at the right time and in the right order to accomplish each task. This complex sequence of events is controlled by

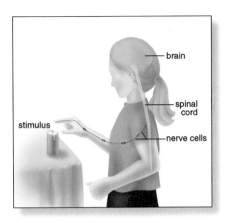

An artist's drawing of how the brain sends messages.

the brain, which acts like a puppet master, telling each muscle when it must contract or expand.

In people with cerebral palsy, the part of the brain that controls the muscles is damaged. Because of this, the muscles may not move in coordination with each other. In some instances they may not move at all. The amount of brain damage varies from person to person. Those with mild forms of cerebral palsy have only a few **symptoms**. Sometimes people may not notice the damage at all.

Sometimes cerebral palsy is so serious that people can not feed themselves and must be fed through a tube in their stomach. Some people with severe cerebral palsy can not move or are unable to control their movements.

There are many different forms of cerebral palsy. Doctors classify cerebral palsy by the parts of the body that are affected. **Hemiplegia** is a form of cerebral palsy that affects one side of a person's body. **Diplegia** affects either both legs or both arms. **Quadriplegia** affects both arms and both legs.

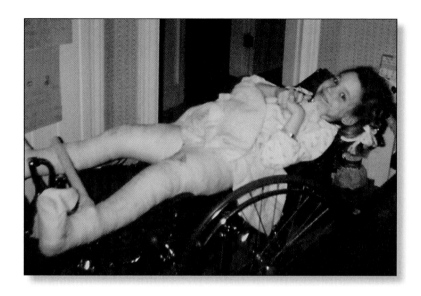

Jennifer Decker, a girl with cerebral palsy, wears a full-body cast after surgery on her hips to turn them outward into a more normal position. She was eight years old at the time.

Physical Effects of Cerebral Palsy

Cerebral palsy causes four types of muscle problems. **Spastic muscles** are rigid and stiff, like those in Austin's legs. Austin's mother said that when Austin's muscles are spastic, his legs become so stiff that they feel as hard as a block of wood. In other instances, the muscles become floppy and weak, or **hypotonic**.

People with cerebral palsy can have trouble controlling their arms or legs. This difficulty is called **athetosis**. People who have problems keeping their balance have a form of the disorder called **ataxic cerebral palsy**.

The lack of muscle control can cause a number of different problems for people with cerebral palsy. If their legs are affected, they may have difficulty walking or not be able to walk at all. If their arms are affected, they may not be able to write, reach for things, or feed themselves. When the muscles of the face and mouth are affected, a person may have trouble speaking or may not be able to speak at all.

Eating can be a big problem for some people with cerebral palsy. Chewing and swallowing require many different muscles to work in coordination with each other. Sometimes the jaw will clench shut just when it should be opening. Other times the tongue may push the food out of the mouth instead of down the throat.

Some people with cerebral palsy can eat only soft foods very slowly. A meal that might take a healthy person a few minutes to eat can take more than an hour for someone with cerebral palsy.

A child with cerebral palsy who has trouble eating may grow more slowly than other children. A child or an adult who cannot eat properly may suffer from **malnutrition** simply because he or she cannot get the food into his or her stomach.

People with cerebral palsy may drool because they cannot control the muscles in their mouth. The poor coordination of their mouth muscles may lead them to inhale food or saliva by accident. This can cause **pneumonia**, which is an infection of the lungs that makes it difficult to breathe. Certain kinds of pneumonia are caused by inhaling food or liquid.

Some people with cerebral palsy have muscles that are so tight they can't move their arms or legs normally. In some forms of spastic cerebral palsy, too-tight muscles may force the legs to turn in at the knees. This causes the person to walk with a jerking motion, called a scissors gait. Muscles that are too tight can twist a person's arm or leg as it grows. Some people with cerebral palsy have hands that are clenched into a fist, caused by tight muscles in the fingers that cause them to curl.

Mental Effects of Cerebral Palsy

Many people with cerebral palsy have the same mental abilities as people without such health problems. But sometimes the brain damage that causes cerebral palsy can affect other areas of brain function in addition to muscle control. Some people with cerebral palsy may be slower to develop mentally. Some may never develop the ability to think abstractly or to be able to solve problems. This is because intellectual development—the ability to think and reason—is connected to physical development. As an infant begins to explore the world physically, his or her mind also begins to develop.

Sometimes brain damage can be so severe that the person is completely disabled and must be cared for by others. In other people with the disorder, the effects may be less severe. They may have a learning disability that makes it harder for them to learn.

Some people with cerebral palsy may appear to be less intelligent than they really are because of their physical appearance. Someone who drools or has trouble communicating because his or her mouth muscles don't work well may not be able to express thoughts so that others can understand what is being said. Other people may think the person has a mental disability when that is not the case.

Carolyn Martin, a woman with severe cerebral palsy, wrote a book about her experiences. For much of her childhood other people thought she was mentally disabled. She had a difficult time speaking, and she drooled, so some people assumed she couldn't understand what was being said. Yet when people took the time to understand her, they discovered she could think as well as anyone else.

In her book, *I Can't Walk So I'll Learn to Dance*, Martin recalls comments from people who toured the school where she and other students with disabilities lived. Many of the visitors "assumed from my physical appearance that my brain worked no better than my hands and feet," she wrote.

Cerebral palsy can interfere with emotional development. The ability to feel happiness and sadness and to experience love and compassion comes from a baby's relationship with other people—other children, parents, and other adults. People often avoid a child who cannot smile or laugh, even though the problem is caused by faulty muscles and is not the child's fault. These children may miss out on being cuddled or having friends because of people's discomfort over the children's looks or acts.

Chapter 3

Causes and Diagnosis

The exact causes of cerebral palsy are not completely known. Although doctors know the disorder is the result of brain damage, they often do not know how the damage occurs.

Certain circumstances are known to be linked to cerebral palsy. Children who are born prematurely, like Austin, are more likely to have the disorder. If problems develop during delivery, the newborn child has a higher risk of having cerebral palsy.

One of the most common causes of brain damage is a lack of oxygen. The brain is made up of millions of special cells. These cells require a good flow of oxygen to survive. When a person is deprived of oxygen, some of the cells in the brain die. When the cells die, that part of the brain no longer works properly.

A fetus—a developing unborn baby—receives its oxygen and nutrients from its mother's blood. The nutrients

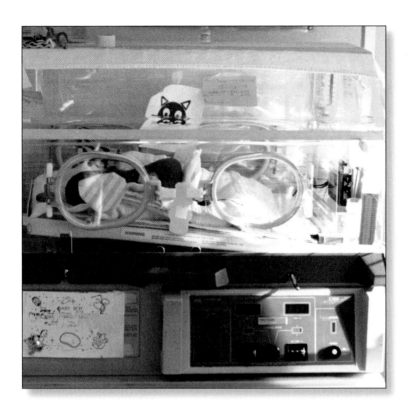

A premature baby lies in a hospital incubator. Babies who are born early are at a greater risk of having cerebral palsy.

and oxygen are carried to the fetus through the **umbilical cord** and into the **placenta**, where the fetus develops and grows. Anything that damages this system can deprive the fetus of oxygen and cause brain damage.

Other problems—such as drug or alcohol use by a pregnant woman—can cause brain damage in the unborn child. In addition, some diseases, such as German measles and **jaundice**, can also cause brain damage.

New Research

In 1998 scientists studying cerebral palsy reported that an infection in the mother of an unborn child may lead to cerebral palsy. The researchers found that blood samples taken from children who were eventually diagnosed with cerebral palsy had higher than normal amounts of a certain kind of **protein** in their bloodstream. These proteins, called **cytokines**, are produced by the body when it is fighting an infection. Cytokines also play a role in the development of the brain in fetuses, including the selection of cells that will eventually become brain cells. Researchers believe high levels of cytokines may be a possible cause of brain damage, although they do not know how the damage occurs.

Diagnosis

Researchers hope that one day they will be able to test the blood of children before they are born to determine if they are at risk for cerebral palsy. As yet, there is no way to predict if children will have the disorder until after they are born. Even then, most of the time a doctor cannot diagnose cerebral palsy until a child is one year old or older. Because there are no tests for cerebral palsy, a doctor must look for symptoms of the disorder that appear as the child develops during the first two years of life.

Infants do not have much control over their arms and legs. They cannot stand up or walk on their own. They can't sit up by themselves or even support their own heads. As children grow older, they begin to develop physically. Their muscles grow stronger and their brains develop to control the muscles.

Doctors know that most children have certain physical abilities, or **motor skills**, at a specific age. For instance, at

At three or four months, most children can reach for a favorite toy. By the time they are one year old or so, most can walk. Children with cerebral palsy, however, take much longer to develop such skills and may never be able to do some things.

three or four months old, children can reach for a favorite toy. Slightly older children, between six and seven months, can sit up by themselves. At eight months, most children are making babbling or cooing sounds. Around the time of a child's first birthday, he or she will be able to stand up and walk.

Although children vary in the age at which they develop these skills, those with cerebral palsy take much longer than normal to walk, talk, and do other activities. Sometimes they never develop these skills. Children with some types of cerebral palsy may not walk until they are eight years old.

A doctor trying to determine if a child has cerebral

palsy must wait and see if that child develops symptoms as he or she grows. If a child is slow to develop certain motor skills, the doctor may suspect the child has cerebral palsy. If this happens, a doctor may have the child's blood tested to check for other possible causes of the delay.

The doctor may also have the child's brain examined by a special X-ray device called a computed tomography (CT) scan. This can show damage to the child's brain that may be slowing development. This damage can be a sign of cerebral palsy.

Doctors can usually diagnose children with severe forms of cerebral palsy—such as quadriplegia—earlier, because their symptoms are more noticeable. It may take longer to diagnose a child with hemiplegia because the symptoms are less severe.

A computer records the results of a patient's CT scan.

Looking Inside the Body: X-rays and CT scans

An X-ray machine uses electromagnetic waves (radiation) to take a picture of the body's insides. The waves leave the machine, pass through the body, and are absorbed by special photographic film on the other side of the body. The waves pass through different tissues inside the body at different rates. These differences mean that certain parts of the film are exposed for a short period of time, while other areas are exposed for a long period. This creates a picture that doctors can use to determine what is inside the body.

A computed tomography (CT) scan is a special type of X-ray machine. It works like an X-ray machine, but it uses a computer to interpret the data. A person undergoing a CT scan lies inside a large machine. An X-ray tube moves around the person, emitting electro-magnetic radiation waves. Instead of film on the other side of the tube, there are special sensors that absorb the radiation particles as they pass through the person. These sensors measure the radiation and feed the information to a computer, which uses the data to create a picture of the inside of the person's body. The CT scan allows doctors to see a cross-section view of the body—as if the person were cut in half.

Seizures

Seizures are another sign that a child may have cerebral palsy. Seizures occur when the brain sends out a burst of uncontrolled electrical signals. These signals cause the body's muscles to twitch and move uncontrollably. Some seizures are small and affect only a small part of the body; for example, causing a person's eye to blink rapidly. Sometimes, however, the whole body is involved. A person having this kind of seizure, called a **grand mal seizure**, falls to the ground and loses consciousness.

There are many causes for seizures besides cerebral palsy. Sometimes a chemical imbalance in a person's brain can cause them. A disorder called **epilepsy** also causes people to have seizures. These problems can often be treated by medication designed to stop the seizures.

Austin's Diagnosis

There were several signs early in Austin's life that led doctors to suspect that he might have cerebral palsy. The first sign was his premature birth. Two weeks after he was born, Austin's doctor performed an **ultrasound** examination on him. An ultrasound is a device that uses sound waves to create a picture of the inside of a person's body. It is similar to an X-ray, except that it measures sound instead of electromagnetic waves.

Because babies who are born prematurely can have brain damage, the doctor wanted to check Austin's brain to see if there was anything wrong. The examination showed that parts of Austin's brain had blood in them, a sign of possible damage. The doctor told Austin's mother that her son might have trouble walking as he got older.

When Austin was four months old, his mother noticed something was different about him. When she put him in her lap, he tried to stand up. His legs were so strong, she recalls, that if he could have balanced himself, he probably could have stood by himself. That stiffness was not normal for a child Austin's age. Austin's mother also noticed that he wasn't developing as quickly as other children his age. Some of those children had begun rolling on the floor and lifting their heads.

Worried, she took Austin to a clinic, where his development could be evaluated. A doctor examined Austin, weighed him, and measured his arms, legs, and head. The doctor asked Austin's mother about his development. After reviewing the information, the doctor recommended that Austin see a physical therapist.

The physical therapist showed Austin's mother how to do a series of stretching exercises with her son that would help reduce the stiffness in Austin's muscles. She also told Austin's mother that she suspected he had cerebral palsy.

The long search for a diagnosis ended with a **neurologist**, a doctor who studies the brain and nervous system. When Austin was nine months old, a neurologist examined him, reviewed his medical records, ordered more scans, and determined that the boy had cerebral palsy.

Chapter 4

Treatment

Cerebral palsy is incurable. The brain damage that causes the disorder cannot be repaired with medication or surgery. Children who have cerebral palsy will have it all their lives.

Doctors and therapists have developed many ways to help people with cerebral palsy live as fully as possible. Medications, surgery, therapy, exercises, and adaptive equipment can all help people cope with cerebral palsy.

The kind of treatment a person with cerebral palsy receives depends on the kind of cerebral palsy he or she has. A person with hemiplegia may need only a brace or special training to use an arm that is bent. Someone with quadriplegia may need many surgeries, adaptive equipment, and therapy to cope with cerebral palsy.

Surgery

Surgery can be used to correct some of the physical deformities caused by cerebral palsy. One common procedure is lengthening the **Achilles tendon**. The Achilles tendon is a piece of tissue on the back of the lower leg that connects the calf muscle to the calcaneus (heel) bone.

In some people with cerebral palsy, the calf muscle is spastic (too tight) and pulls the heel upward, causing them to walk on tiptoe. A surgeon can lengthen the tendon, allowing the person to walk more normally.

Another common surgery lengthens the muscles in the hips. Some people with cerebral palsy have muscles on the inside of the upper leg that are so tight they actually pull the leg bone out of its socket in the hip bone. To correct this, the doctor cuts some of the muscles in the groin area. This allows the muscles to relax. As the muscles heal they become longer and produce less pressure on the legs.

Sometimes the bones of a person with cerebral palsy may not grow in correct alignment because they are being pulled by tight muscles. For instance, a leg may be twisted so that the foot points to one side. To fix this, a surgeon cuts the bone, then aligns it correctly. Another surgical technique involves cutting the nerves to certain muscles. This blocks the signal from the brain to the muscle and allows it to relax.

Medication

Although cerebral palsy itself cannot be treated by medication, some of its effects can be reduced by certain drugs. A person who has seizures, for example, can take medications that help control the seizures. Medications that relax tight muscles and allow people to use an arm or a leg normally can be injected directly into the muscle. This kind of treatment doesn't last long, however, and may have to be repeated every four to six months. It is a painful treatment and must be done while the person is under anesthesia.

Braces

Various kinds of braces are used to help straighten limbs that are bent or twisted. Braces can also be used to provide support for weak muscles. Many of these braces are made of thin plastic and are worn under clothing. Other people may not even notice that the person is wearing a brace.

An **ankle-foot orthosis** is a brace worn on the foot and lower leg. It is used on children who have tight muscles in their calves that cause them to walk on tiptoe. The brace forces their foot into a flattened position so they can walk normally. Another kind of brace is used for children whose fingers curl into a fist. The brace holds the hand open. Although braces don't cure the problem, they keep tight muscles from getting tighter and prevent them from causing more problems as the child grows older.

Therapy

There are two major kinds of therapy used to treat patients with cerebral palsy: physical and occupational. Physical therapists teach patients to exercise arms and legs that otherwise might never be used. Physical therapy for people with cerebral palsy is most important when they are young. As children get older, physical therapy becomes less important.

To encourage children to exercise, physical therapists try

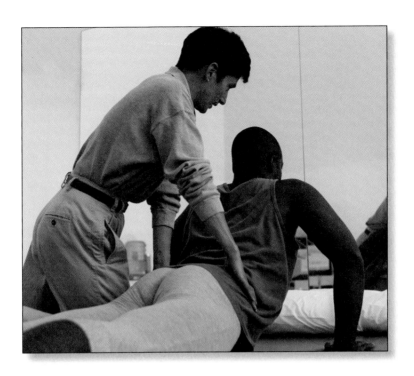

A physical therapist helps a young man with his exercises.

to make therapy sessions fun by playing games that require young patients to move their arms and legs. Physical therapy can include more than just simple exercises. Learning how to ride a horse or a bicycle, ballet dancing, gymnastics, or karate lessons are often used as forms of physical therapy.

Occupational therapists teach people how to live with disabilities and show them ways around their physical limitations. For example, an occupational therapist may show a person with a bent arm how to eat using special utensils or how to tie shoe laces with a special knot that doesn't require both hands.

As children with cerebral palsy grow older, occupational therapists teach them skills they will need to live on their own. Learning how to drive using a specially equipped van with hand controls or how to type on a computer keyboard are among the lessons an occupational therapist provides.

A specialist called a speech therapist works with people whose cerebral palsy makes it difficult for them to talk. A speech therapist teaches people how to shape the mouth to form words. Austin's speech therapist teaches him short words and hand signals he can use to communicate. His therapist also works with Austin's mother to help her understand her son.

Chapter 5

Living With Cerebral Palsy

M any people with cerebral palsy live normal lives. They grow up, go to college, find jobs, get married, and have children. Other people may not even know that those with mild forms of cerebral palsy have the disorder.

For others with cerebral palsy, however, living a normal life may be more difficult. Those who have serious physical disabilities that make it difficult to walk or talk may have trouble getting into college or finding a job. If cerebral palsy affects their mental capabilities, they may never be able to live on their own.

Even those with serious disabilities, though, can often overcome them by using special equipment such as wheelchairs, braces, and devices that help them communicate.

New laws make life easier for people with disabilities. The Americans with Disabilities Act, passed by the United States Congress in 1990, prevents employers from refusing to hire disabled people simply because they are disabled. It also requires businesses, public transportation, restaurants, and stores to be accessible to people with physical disabilities. An employer with a disabled employee must make an effort to help that person do his or her job. This could mean providing special equipment needed to do a job or modifying a work area for the disabled person.

Jennifer Decker is a twenty-one-year-old college student with cerebral palsy that affects the left side of her body. The muscles in her left hand and leg are so tight that she has trouble making them do what she wants them to do. She can walk with a crutch, but it is difficult for her.

Jennifer lives by herself in an apartment on her college's campus. She is studying psychology and hopes to become a counselor after she finishes her education. Jennifer has adapted her life to accommodate her physical limitations. Her apartment has a ramp leading to the front door, which makes it easier for her to enter and leave the building. She rides an electric scooter around campus. She also takes the scooter to the mall when she goes shopping.

Education

The kind of education a student with cerebral palsy receives depends on the seriousness of his or her disability. Children with cerebral palsy who have normal brain function can attend regular classes in public or private schools along with other students who do not have such health problems.

Those with severe physical or mental disabilities often need an aide. Aides are trained to help students learn while they attend regular classes. Most public schools have special classrooms for students with severe disabilities. Some students may have all their classes in the special rooms with teachers trained to work with them. Other students may attend some of their classes in the special classroom and have other classes with the rest of the school's students.

Jennifer Decker during her senior year of high school.

Many teachers believe students with cerebral palsy learn better in classrooms with nondisabled children. In an article written in a magazine for teachers, one teacher told a story about a student she called Dustin. Dustin, who was six, was seriously affected by cerebral palsy. He wore a steel brace on one leg, could not speak or read, and had seizures. While he was in this teacher's class, however, Dustin learned to sing and read aloud with the other students.

Jennifer attended public schools through eighth grade, then enrolled in a private high school. An aide helped her in wood shop and home economics classes. Jennifer's parents, school officials, and therapists put together a plan designed especially to meet Jennifer's needs. The plan listed what changes her teachers could make to allow Jennifer to do her best. For example, Jennifer was given extra time to take tests because she has difficulty writing.

Jennifer says she never felt different from other children until she began attending school. She remembers limping slowly along the hallway while other children ran past her on their way to recess. As an elementary and middle school student, Jennifer says she often felt singled out because of her disability. She had to leave her classes several times a week to take part in physical and occupational therapy sessions. Often she had to make up the classwork she missed at home.

Jennifer also had to endure teasing from other students who made fun of the way she walked. As a young child, she had to ride in a special bus to and from school, which also made her feel different from the other students.

Jennifer says growing up with cerebral palsy and the treatment she received from others made her shy and prevented her from developing good social skills. She said she has few close friends and is uncomfortable about introducing herself to other people.

Despite this, Jennifer has made an effort to take part in the society around her. In high school she was in student government and she also helped to plan religious services at a Catholic school she attended. Jennifer speaks to students who are studying physical and occupational therapy at her college, to teach them how to help people with disabilities.

Communication and Aids to Living

People with cerebral palsy who have trouble speaking, or who cannot speak at all, sometimes communicate by using simple hand signals or eye signals. Children who are unable to move their heads can move their eyes to signal "yes" or "no" replies to questions.

When he was younger, Austin used a **communication board** that had pictures of everyday items on it. When he wanted a certain object, Austin pointed to its picture on the board. More sophisticated versions of the boards have a computerized voice that speaks when the person presses a button.

People with cerebral palsy who can't move their arms or hands can use a specially designed light strapped to the head to select items on a computerized communication board. The person activates the board by using his or her head to direct the light to the desired spot.

For people who can speak but cannot use their arms, there are computer programs that understand the human voice. These programs, which run on ordinary personal computers, print out words as they are spoken. When Jennifer takes exams, she uses a computer like this so she can speak her answers instead of trying to type them.

Specially trained dogs help some people with cerebral palsy perform the tasks of everyday living. These dogs, called **service dogs**, are trained to perform tasks that are difficult for people with disabilities, such as opening doors and picking objects off the floor. The dogs can even pay a store clerk from a specially designed wallet.

Recreation

Many people with cerebral palsy enjoy sports just as other people do. Bicycle riding, horseback riding, and swimming are among the activities that people with cerebral palsy pursue. Special equipment helps people with disabilities to enjoy sports. Jennifer Decker has skied since she was in sixth grade. She uses a bi-ski, which consists of two skis attached to a seat. She sits on the seat and skis down the mountain. Volunteers ski in front and behind to guide her along the slope.

Jennifer, in her bi-ski, skis down a slope at Sunday River ski resort in Maine in 1998.

Some people with cerebral palsy lift weights. A California man who has cerebral palsy began body-building to improve his physical condition. When he started, he weighed 117 pounds and could not lift ten pounds with his legs, which he had trouble controlling. After exercising with weights, he weighed 140 pounds and was able to lift several times his own weight using his legs. He entered a bodybuilding contest and won a second-place award, beating competitors who were not disabled. His exercising also paid off by improving his balance.

Living Independently

Many people who have cerebral palsy live on their own, even those who have moderate physical disabilities. Wheelchairs, crutches, and other devices help them adapt their life to whatever physical limits they may have.

One man who had hemiplegia that affected his right arm and hand became a computer program systems analyst, married, and had three children. By making certain adjustments, he learned how to carry his children, play golf, swim, water ski, snow ski, and sail.

For people whose cerebral palsy affects their mobility, however, the challenges can be great. They may have difficulty getting into some buildings. Their homes must be specially designed or modified to allow them to get around easily. They may need special controls to be able to drive their cars. People who don't drive must rely on public transportation that has been specially equipped to carry people with disabilities.

Jennifer can use her right leg when driving. A knob on the steering wheel of her car helps her grip and turn the wheel with her right hand. Jennifer's car has also been modified so that the turn signal control is on the right-hand side instead of the left.

Some people with cerebral palsy require help with everyday tasks, such as dressing, bathing, and eating. Those with serious physical or mental disabilities may always have to live with people who can help them. Parents of children with severe cerebral palsy may have to care for their offspring long after they have become adults. Others live in **group homes** after they reach adulthood and are cared for by specially trained staff members.

A few people who are severely affected by cerebral palsy cannot live in a group home. Their physical and mental disabilities are so serious that they must live in a nursing home or other facility where they can get full-time care.

Life Span

Improved medical care allows most children with cerebral palsy to survive to adulthood. Ninety percent of children with mild forms of cerebral palsy live to become adults. Children with more serious forms of cerebral palsy, such as quadriplegia, have a lower survival rate, about 70 percent.

The majority of people with cerebral palsy live as long as other people do. But they may suffer from medical problems related to the disease. And they may feel the effects of aging—such as developing arthritis—earlier than other people.

One of the greatest risks for children with cerebral palsy is pneumonia and other respiratory diseases. Many of these children have trouble swallowing and can inhale food or saliva into their lungs. This can cause pneumonia, a disease that makes it hard for them to breathe and that can be fatal.

What the Future Holds

As Austin grew older, his speech improved. By the time he was four years old, he no longer needed a communication board. In fact, his mother said, "There is no limit on the words that are coming out of his mouth." But he still can not walk or sit by himself.

As a child with quadriplegic cerebral palsy, Austin will have many challenges as he grows older. No one knows whether he will be able to walk on his own or live by himself when he becomes an adult. His mother says she does not look too far into the future but sets daily goals for

Jennifer Decker moves into her dorm room at the beginning of her sophomore year at the University of New England in Biddeford, Maine. Her stepfather, Mick Carroll, helps with the move.

Austin. She hopes he will grow up to accept his disability and appreciate the talents he has in order to lead a fulfilling life.

"I take it one goal at a time," she said.

Jennifer Decker, too, takes each day as it comes. She has learned to adapt to her disability and has plans for a full life. But even with adaptations, she faces many difficulties every day that people without disabilities never consider. For instance, she uses the drive-up window at her bank because of the difficulty she has walking. But because she has trouble with her left arm and hand, she has to reach across her body with her right arm to use the window. This has caused her to drop money on the ground at least once.

Jennifer cannot fit her scooter in the car she drives. If she goes someplace where she will need the scooter, someone else has to bring it in a car or van. She hopes someday to buy a specially equipped van that will let her load and transport the scooter by herself.

And despite laws that require public buildings to be accessible, there are still many places Jennifer cannot go. At her school, she sometimes has trouble visiting friends who live in dormitories that are not accessible to people with disabilities. But Jennifer doesn't give up easily. After having difficulty getting into the school's campus center, she convinced college officials to install doors that open automatically.

Jennifer wants to become a counselor and work with children who have disabilities. "A lot of people don't realize the psychological stuff you go through when you are disabled," she said. She plans to use her own experiences to help others who have similar problems.

Further Reading

Books

Aaseng, Nathan. *Cerebral Palsy*. New York: Franklin Watts, 1991.

Bergman, Thomas. *Going Places: Children Living With Cerebral Palsy*. Milwaukee, Wisc.: Gareth Stevens Inc., 1991.

Geralis, Elaine, ed. *Children with Cerebral Palsy, A Parent's Guide*. Bethesda, Md.: Woodbine House, 1998.

Kriegsman, Kay H., et al. *Taking Charge: Teenagers Talk About Life & Physical Disabilities*. Bethesda, Md.: Woodbine House, 1993.

Levine, Melvin D. *Keeping a Head in School: A Student's Book About Learning Abilities & Learning Disorders*. Cambridge, Mass.: Educators Publishing Service, 1999.

Martin, Carolyn, with Gregg Lewis. *I Can't Walk So I'll Learn to Dance*. Grand Rapids, Mich.: Zondervan Publishing House, 1994.

Nixon, Shelley. *From Where I Sit: Making My Way with Cerebral Palsy*. Madison, Wisc.: Turtleback Books, 1999.

Pimm, Paul. *Living With Cerebral Palsy*. Austin, Texas: Raintree/Steck-Vaughn, 1999.

Schleichkorn, Jay. *Coping With Cerebral Palsy: Answers to Questions Parents Often Ask*. Austin, Texas: Pro-Ed, 1993.

White, Peter. *Disabled People.* New York: Franklin Watts, 1990.

Newsletters

Open Hearts, Open Minds, Open Doors. Pathways Awareness Foundation, 123 N. Wacker Drive, Suite 900, Chicago, IL 60606, (800) 955-2445; <http://www.pathwaysawareness.org>

For More Information

The following is a list of resources and Web sites that deal with cerebral palsy.

Organizations

American Academy for Cerebral Palsy and Developmental Medicine
6300 North River Road, Suite 727, Rosemont, IL 60018-4226, (847) 698 1635; <http://www.aacpdm.org>

Children's Association for Maximum Potential
P.O. Box 27086, San Antonio, TX 78227, (210) 292-3566, (210) 292-3567; <http://www.serve.com/campcamp/index01.htm>

Independent Living Research Utilization Project (ILRU) The Institute for Rehabilitation and Research
2323 South Shepherd, Suite 1000, Houston, TX 77019; (713) 520-0232, (713) 520-5136 (TDD); <http://www.bcm.tmc.edu/ilru>

March of Dimes Birth Defects Foundation
1275 Mamaroneck Avenue, White Plains, NY 10605, (888) 663-4637, (914) 428-7100; <http://www.modimes.org>

National Association of Developmental Disabilities Councils
1234 Massachusetts Avenue NW, Suite 103,

Washington, DC 20005; (202) 347-1234; <http://www.igc.apc.org/NADDC>

National Easter Seals Society, Inc.

230 West Monroe Street, Suite 1800, Chicago, IL 60606, (800) 221-6827, (312) 726-6200, (312) 726-4258 (TTY); <http://www.easterseals.org>

National Information Center for Children and Youth with Disabilities

P.O. Box 1492, Washington, DC 20013-1492; (800) 695-0285; <http://www.nichcy.org>

National Institute of Neurological Disorders and Stroke

Offices of Public Liaison, NIH Neurological Institute, P.O. Box 5801, Bethesda, MD 20892; (301) 496-4000, (800) 352-9424; <http://www.ninds.nih.gov/health_ and_medical/disorders/cerebral_palsy.htm>

National Rehabilitation Information Center (NARIC)

1010 Wayne Ave., Suite 800, Silver Spring, MD 20910; (800) 346-2742, (301) 562-2400, (301) 495-5626 (TT); <http://www.naric.com>

Pathways Awareness Foundation

123 N. Wacker Drive, Suite 900, Chicago, IL 60606, (800) 955-2445; <http://www.pathwaysawareness.org>

United Cerebral Palsy Associations, Inc.

1660 L Street, NW, Suite 700, Washington, DC 20036-5602, (800) USA-5-UCP, (202) 776-0406, (202) 973-7197 (TTY); <http://www.ucpa.org>

United States Cerebral Palsy Athletic Association

25 W. Independence Way, Kingston, RI 02881, (401) 792-7130; <http://www.uscpaa.org>

Internet Resources

<http://kidshealth.org/kid/health_problems/cerebral_palsy.html>
KidsHealth, run by The Nemours Foundation

<http://familydoctor.org>
Site of the American Academy of Family Physicians

<http://www.drkoop.com/conditions/cerebralpalsy>
Site of C. Everett Koop, former U.S. Surgeon General

<http://www.people.virginia.edu/~mon-grow>
Cerebral Palsy: A Multimedia Tutorial from the
Children's Medical Center, University of Virginia

<http://www.ninds.nih.gov/health_and_medical/pubs/cerebral_palsyhtr.htm>
Cerebral Palsy—Hope Through Research from the
U.S. National Institute of Neurological Disorders and
Stroke

<http://www.childrenwithdisabilities.ncjrs.org>
The Children With Disabilities Web site

<http://www.irsc.org/cp.htm>
Internet Resources for Special Children Web site

<http://www.kidsource.com/nichcy/cerebral_palsy.html>
Site of the National Information Center for Children
and Youth with Disabilities

Glossary

Achilles tendon—A piece of tissue that connects the muscles in the calf of the leg to the bone of the heel.

ankle-foot orthosis—A brace that helps align the ankle and the foot.

ataxic cerebral palsy—A form of cerebral palsy in which a person's sense of balance is impaired.

athetosis—A syndrome marked by constant, uncontrolled movement of a limb.

cerebral palsy—A disorder marked by the inability of the brain to control muscular movement properly.

communication board—A device with pictures of everyday objects on it used to help communicate.

cytokine—A chemical produced by the body in response to an infection.

diagnosis—The conclusion reached after investigating the symptoms of a disease.

diplegia—A form of cerebral palsy that affects either both legs or both arms.

epilepsy—A disorder marked by interruptions in brain activity that causes seizures.

grand mal seizure—A type of seizure in which the person falls to the ground and may lose consciousness.

group home—A living situation where several people can live with help from professional counselors.

hemiplegia—A type of cerebral palsy that affects one side of the body.

hypotonic muscles—Muscles that lack tone or are weak and floppy.

jaundice—A condition that gives the skin a yellowish color.

malnutrition—A condition in which the body doesn't get enough of the food needed for life and growth.

motor skills—A list of physical capabilities.

muscle—Tissue in the body that connects and moves bones.

neurologist—A doctor who specializes in nerves.

occupational therapist—A health professional who helps teach people with disabilities how to adapt their lifestyle.

physical therapist—A health professional who treats people by using exercises and mechanical devices.

placenta—An organ that connects the developing fetus with the mother's body.

pneumonia—A disease marked by inflammation of the lungs.

protein—A chemical compound in living creatures that combines to create tissues (such as skin and muscle) as well as other compounds needed by the body.

quadriplegia—A condition that affects all four limbs of the body.

seizure—A sudden, temporary change in the normal electrical activity of the brain that affects how a person thinks and acts.

service dogs—Dogs trained to help disabled people.

spastic muscles—Muscles that are constantly tense.

speech therapist—A medical professional who helps people with speaking problems.

symptoms—Physical and mental effects of a disease or disorder.

ultrasound—A method of viewing the interior of the body using sound waves.

umbilical cord—A piece of tissue carrying blood vessels that connects a fetus to the placenta.

Index

Achilles tendon, 25
adaptive equipment, 24, 29, 30,
    34; *See also* braces,
    communication devices,
    wheelchairs.
Americans with Disabilities Act,
    29–30
athetosis, 12
braces, 24, 25, 29, 31
brain, 6, 9, 10–11, 14–15, 16,
    18, 20, 22-23, 24–25, 30
brain damage, 6, 11, 14, 16–18,
    20, 22, 23, 24
cerebral palsy,
    causes of, 6, 11, 14, 16–18, 24
    coping with, 7, 8, 24, 27,
        29–38
    diagnosis of, 7, 18–23
    statistics, 6
    symptoms of, 5–7, 11–15,
        18–20, 22–23, 29, 30–32,
        36
    treatments, 24-28; *See also*
        occupational therapy,
        physical therapy, speech
        therapy, surgery.
    types of, 11–12, 13, 19, 20,
        29, 36
childhood development, 14,
    18–20, 23
communication devices, 8, 28,
    29, 32–33, 36
computed tomography (CT)
    scan, 20, 21
computers, 28, 33, 35
cytokines, 18
Decker, Jennifer, 30–32, 33, 34,
    35, 37–38

development group, 8
diplegia, 11
Dustin, 31
eating difficulties, 6, 13, 27, 35
education, 15, 30–32, 38
emotional effects, 15
employment, 29–30, 38
epilepsy, 22
exercise, 7–8, 23, 24, 26–27
group homes, 35
hemiplegia, 11, 20, 24, 35
life span, 36
Little, William, 9
malnutrition, 13
Martin, Carolyn, 15
medication, 22, 24, 25–26
mental effects, 14–15, 29, 30,
    35
motor skills, 18, 20
muscles, 6, 7, 9–15, 18, 22, 23,
    25–26, 30
    hypotonic, 12
    spastic, 12–13, 25
Nelon, Shana, 5–8, 12, 23, 28,
    36
nerves, 10, 25
neurologist, 23
occupational therapy, 26–28, 32
physical effects, 5–8, 12–14, 15,
    23, 29, 30, 32, 34–35
physical therapy, 7, 8, 23, 24,
    26–27, 32
pneumonia, 13, 36
quadriplegia, 11, 20, 24, 36
recreation, 33–34
research, 17–18
Robertson, Austin, 5–8, 12, 16,
    22–23, 28, 33, 36–37

scissors gait, 13
seizures, 22, 25, 31
service dogs, 33
speech therapy, 7–8, 28
surgery, 24–25
ultrasound, 22
wheelchairs, 6, 29, 34
X-ray, 20, 21, 22

AAZ -2525